D1373178

CHRISTMAS WREATHS & GARLANDS

Chris Rankin

A Sterling/Lark Book
Sterling Publishing Co., Inc.   New York

Editor: Carol Taylor
Art Director: Geri Camarda
Photography: Evan Bracken
Production: Elaine Thompson

Library of Congress Cataloging-in-Publication Data
Available

10 9 8 7 6 5 4 3 2 1

A Sterling/Lark Book

Published by Sterling Publishing Co., Inc.
387 Park Ave. South, New York, NY 10016

Created and produced by Altamont Press, Inc.
50 College St., Asheville, NC 28801

© 1994, Altamont Press

Distributed in Canada by Sterling Publishing,
c/o Canadian Manda Group, P.O. Box 920, Station U, Toronto,
        Ontario, Canada M8Z 5P9
Distributed in Great Britain and Europe by Cassell PLC, Villiers House,
        41/47 Strand, London WC2N 5JE, England
Distributed in Australia by Capricorn Link (Australia) Pty Ltd.,
P.O.Box 6651, Baulkham Hills, Business Centre, NSW 2153, Australia

ISBN 0-8069-1279-0

Contents

Making Wreaths: The Basics

Christmas wreaths are as traditional as boughs of holly, as festive as sprigs of mistletoe, and as easy to make as New Year's resolutions. On the front door, they welcome family and friends with promises of good company and good times. In living room and dining room, bedroom and guest room, they lift the spirits and celebrate the season. When we plan to deck the halls, we think of wreaths.

Even if you have no craft experience whatever, making a wreath is the perfect way to add your own creative touch to your holiday home. Nothing could be simpler. You don't need advanced degrees or special powers—just a few tools and materials, a couple of evenings, and a conviction that in the vast territory between "perfect" and "ugly," there's lots of room to maneuver.

Essentially, a wreath is a collection of materials arranged in a circle and hung on a wall…or on a door, mantle, cabinet, or window. You have only to select your materials, attach them to a wreath base, and collect the compliments.

FINDING MATERIALS

Craft stores. If you haven't wandered down the aisles of a large craft store recently, it's worth a trip. Here's what you're likely to find:

Dried flowers, real and artificial, in every imaginable color, shape, and size.

Preserved foliage, such as cedar and magnolia leaves.

Pods from practically every plant that produces seeds, imported from all over the world, ready to be spray-painted or used their natural color: round, exotic lotus pods...long, oval mahogany pods...okra pods...eucalyptus pods that resemble tiny jingle bells...and pods even the store owner won't be able to identify.

Dried fruit (pomegranates, orange slices, apple slices).

Ornaments and knickknacks: ceramic birds, straw bird's nests, tiny cottages, white-washed twigs, glitter, paint, small gold stars, and so on.

Ribbons and ready-made bows in an incredible variety of colors, patterns, and materials. Don't overlook the long strings of beading in different hues.

Artificial evergreen wreaths and garlands, ready to decorate with your own materials.

Craft berries in various colors, sizes, and textures.

Feathers in natural and unnatural hues.

And dozens of other things.

House and yard. Evergreen trees or shrubs can be pruned for their fragrant clippings, and the delicate twigs from winter-dead trees make handsome wreath bases. Moss can be gathered from your yard (or purchased from a florist).

If you have a favorite Christmas ornament or decoration—a gorgeous parchment angel, for example, or even a child's well-loved teddy bear—you can display it to advantage on a wreath.

Woods and pastures. A leisurely walk on a winter afternoon can

provide all kinds of materials: pods, lichens, rose hips, twigs, moss, evergreens, even abandoned nests.

Et cetera. Some discount marts have well-stocked craft departments—excellent sources of wreath bases and tools. At Christmas time, fabric stores carry good selections of ribbons.

BASES

Wreath bases are universally available at craft stores and discount marts. The kind of base you select will depend on the type and abundance of your materials and on the kind of look you desire.

Straw. Whether it's 8 or 20 inches (20 or 50 cm) in diameter, a straw base is broad and bulky, an excellent choice when you have lots of materials and want a full, lush wreath. It accepts picks and pins readily and holds them securely (see "Means of Attachment").

Moss. Wire frames or straw bases covered with Spanish moss are attractive, ready-to-use bases.

Grapevine. Vine bases can also support lush foliage and flowers, although attaching materials takes a little more care. Since vine bases are good-looking, parts of them can be left bare, especially with natural materials.

Wire. Wire bases are essentially two circles attached to each other with cross pieces. They are excellent supports for heavy materials, such as evergreen branches. Also available are single wire rings.

Twig. Increasingly popular, twig bases are fascinating. Since the only reason to use one is to display it—that is, to leave parts of it bare—it's a good choice when you don't have an abundant supply of decorative materials.

MEANS OF ATTACHMENT

Simple wreath-making tools are sold in craft stores and discount marts.

Glue gun. A glue gun may not be the most fun you can have for under $10, but it's close. Fast, easy to use, and incredibly versatile, it can affix almost anything to almost anything else.

Three suggestions: First, don't hesitate to use as much glue as you need. Some of the wreaths in this book contain hidden globs the size of golf balls. Second, hold a freshly glued object in position for a few seconds, until the glue sets. Third, low-melt glue guns—which use glue sticks that melt at a lower temperature—are less likely to burn your fingers than the high-melt ones.

Floral picks. A floral pick looks like an over-grown toothpick with a flexible wire attached to one end. The pick acts as an artificial stem. Its sharp end penetrates a variety of bases—foam, straw, herb, vine—and holds upright and stable whatever flimsy plant or odd-shaped item is attached to it. For extra security, put a dab of hot glue on the end of a pick before inserting it, especially on a vine base.

To attach a flower or leaf to a pick, hold the pick and the plant's stem together and wrap the wire tightly around both stem and pick, spiraling down the entire length of both. If you like, wrap flexible *floral tape* around the picked stem. Attach a round or odd-shaped item to a pick with hot glue.

Floral wire. Inexpensive, flexible, and green, floral wire is sold in two forms. Spool wire is a finer gauge, appropriate for holding bows together and for wiring delicate materials. The stiffer wire sold in precut lengths is excellent for sturdier work, such as making a loop for hanging a wreath or piercing a crab apple in order to wire it to a base. Both types of wire can be cut with shears or heavy scissors.

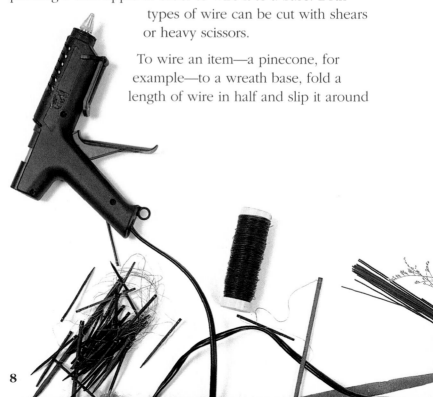

To wire an item—a pinecone, for example—to a wreath base, fold a length of wire in half and slip it around the cone, between two layers of petals. Twist the wire ends together several times right next to the cone. Wrap the wire ends around the base and twist them together again. On a vine base, wire the object to any handy strand of vine.

Floral pins. A U-shaped floral pin is simple to use. Just place its ends on either side of the material to be attached and push the pin into the base.

MAKING BOWS

Some wreaths seem to demand a bow, and most craft stores will make one for you from any ribbon you buy. If yours won't, fear not. To make a large bow, simply form as many loops as you want and wire them together around the center with spool wire. Then wire the bow to the base. Wired ribbon—which has a wire running along each edge—is especially easy to manipulate.

Keep in mind that bows use up enormous amounts of ribbon—4 to 8 yards (3.7 to 7.4 m) of it, depending on the size of the bow. A simple two-loop bow (the kind used to tie shoelaces) is often effective and uses far less ribbon.

DESIGNING A WREATH

Considering the beauty of the materials—evergreens, ribbons, dried flowers—it's hard to go wrong. A short checklist will help you decide how to select materials and how to arrange them on the base.

Color. Although red and green wreaths are wonderful, feel free to venture into the rest of the spectrum. Pastels make interesting changes of pace in a red-and-green world, and all-white wreaths can be stunning.

A wreath can boast variations of the same color—10 different shades of red, for example—or a riot of contrasting hues. Determine where the wreath will hang, and coordinate it with its surroundings.

Angle. Consider the angle at which you're attaching materials to the base. The most popular approach is to insert all the materials at the same angle, creating a spiral design (see the wreath on page 40). Alternatively, if you have a great many materials and plan a very full wreath, you can attach them at different angles for a hodgepodge effect (see the wreath on page 32).

Sectioning. One approach is to mentally divide the base into three concentric circles: the outer rim, the front face, and the inner rim. Materials can then be applied in three rings (see the yarrow wreath on page 20).

Random design. Some of the most interesting wreaths are based on a simple technique: attaching each material randomly to the base, making sure that each material is fairly evenly distributed around the wreath.

ABOUT THE WREATHS IN THIS BOOK

The 27 projects in this book—mostly wreaths, with an occasional garland and swag—fall into five broad categories: evergreen wreaths; wreaths that feature dried flowers; culinary wreaths; wreaths in which the base itself is central to the design; and wreaths that feature a favorite knickknack or ornament.

While you can certainly replicate any wreath you're particularly fond of, you can also use them as inspiration for your own creations.

In making your own wreaths, *substitute, substitute, substitute.* If a wreath uses one kind of red flower and you can't find it or don't like it, look around for other red flowers that will please you as much or more. If you don't like gold-bordered white brocade ribbon, find another one that you do like. If you can't find (or don't want to use) a 21-inch (53 cm) wreath base, use a different size.

ENCOURAGING WORDS

If you're still wary about making a Christmas wreath, one final thought: Good will really does abound this time of year. And guests who are mildly besotted with brotherhood are not going to notice that the third pine cone from the left on your holiday wreath is slightly askew.

So put on the tea kettle, turn on the carols, get out the glue gun, and embark on an adventure that will enliven your entire holiday season.

Christmas Cones and Greenery

Materials: *16-inch (40 cm) wire base; long cones; sprigs of spruce, cedar, fir, pine, and boxwood (or other evergreens); 5 yards (4.6 m) of wired ribbon 2 to 3 inches (5 to 8 cm) wide; spool wire; glue gun*

To make the body of the wreath, form bunches of spruce and wire them onto the base by their stems. Point the tips of the foliage in a clockwise direction all the way around the base, so that the foliage of each bunch overlaps the stems of the previous one. Cover the front, outside rim, and inside edge completely. This wreath looks best when very full; don't skimp on any of the greenery.

Hot-glue stems of the other greenery around the wreath, working with one type at a time and distributing it evenly around the front, outside, and inside of the wreath. Again, point the tips clockwise, following the spiral design.

Wire the cones onto the wreath. Make a bow with one streamer about 1-1/2 yards (1.3 m) long. Wire the bow to the top of the wreath and drape the streamer around the front, tucking it into the greenery in several places.

Birch Bark Wreath

Materials: *moss-covered straw base, grapevines, preserved cedar, pinecones, ribbon, pomegranates, red craft berries, strips of birch bark, German statice (the small white flowers), lichens, fresh Fraser fir or other fragrant evergreens, floral pins, floral picks, spool wire, glue gun*

Lay the grapevines around the front of the base so that the vine makes three or four complete circles, and pin the vine in place.

Cluster pieces of cedar on picks and insert them into the base, making sure all the tips point in a counterclockwise direction. Wire the pinecones to large picks and distribute them evenly around the wreath. Encircle the wreath with ribbon, weaving it in and out of other materials, and pin it in place. Hot-glue on the pomegranates and pick in the berry clusters, with the berries angled counterclockwise. Hot-glue pieces of birch bark around the wreath, tucking it under other materials here and there. Hot-glue the lichens and the German statice in place, then pick in sprigs of Fraser fir. The statice and fir should maintain the counter-clockwise spiral design.

Evergreen Garland

Materials: *about 40 sprigs
each of white pine, hemlock,
blue juniper, and evergreen
japonica (or other mixed
greens); dried white flowers;
Sweet Annie; spool wire; heavy-
gauge wire or macrame cord*

This simple garland displays four
different shades of green. To make it,
form bundles of each material by wiring about
six sprigs together by their stems, using spool
wire. Then cut a 6-foot (1.8 m) "spine" of heavy
wire or cord. Wire the bundles to the spine,
pointing them in the same direction and
distributing them evenly.

Holly Swag

Materials: *branches of holly, branches of fir or spruce, red velvet bow, spool wire*

Nothing could be simpler than this traditional, festive swag. Arrange the holly and the evergreens in a fan shape and wire them together by their stems. Form a loop with the wire ends, for hanging. Wire a bow to the stems, covering the wires.

Cedar, Juniper, and Lilies

Materials: moss-covered straw base, sprigs of preserved juniper with blue berries attached, cedar sprigs, mahonia (or other saw-toothed leaves), Sweet Annie, dried white lilies, dried white larkspur (including some new growth), eucalyptus leaves, floral picks, glue gun

Although this wreath is incredibly full and lush, the spiral pattern is still apparent. All materials are arranged in clusters, with their tips pointing in a clockwise direction.

First attach clusters of greenery to floral picks and insert them into the base: the juniper, then the cedar, then the saw-toothed leaves of mahonia. (If mahonia is not available, substitute holly or other preserved leaves.) Cover the base fully, including the outside rim and inner opening.

Working with one piece at a time, cover the stems of the remaining materials with hot glue and insert them into the wreath, arranging them in clusters: first the reddish brown Sweet Annie, then the lilies, the larkspur, and the pale, oval eucalyptus leaves.

Boxwood, Berries, and Pods

Materials: *12- or 14-inch (30 or 35 cm) wire ring, sprigs of boxwood, okra pods, lotus pods, mahogany pods, stalks of wheat, red craft berries, gold spray paint, spool wire, glue gun*

Spray-paint the okra pods gold and set them aside to dry.

Form the body of the wreath by wiring bunches of boxwood around the wire ring, pointing the tips of all foliage in a clockwise direction; the foliage of each bunch should overlap the stems of the previous one. Cover the front, outside rim, and inside opening completely.

Hot-glue four okra pods into the lower left of the wreath, pointing them upward and to the left, as shown. Trim the wheat stalks so that their different lengths make up an attractive bundle. Wire the stems together and hot-glue the bundle in place. Hot-glue the round lotus pods, then the oval mahogany pods to the bottom of the wreath. Then hot-glue sprigs of craft berries around the wreath, clustering most of them near the lotus pods. Finally, hot-glue the remaining okra pod to the bottom of the wreath, so that it projects outward.

Golden Yarrow Wreath

Materials: 21-inch (52 cm) artificial evergreen wreath, pearly everlasting (or other dried white flowers), dried pomegranates, dried heads of yarrow, dried orange slices, nandina berries, floral picks, glue gun

Bend the tips of the evergreen branches until they are evenly spaced and orderly.

Three rings of materials encircle this wreath. To establish the outer ring, make eight bouquets of pearly everlasting about 4 inches (10 cm) long and 4 inches in diameter. Attach them to floral picks, dab some hot glue on the ends of the picks, and insert them at intervals just inside the outer rim of the wreath. Hot-glue the yarrow heads between the bunches of pearly everlasting.

For the center ring, hot-glue the pomegranates around the center of the wreath, placing each one directly opposite a bouquet of pearly everlasting.

For the inner ring, make ten 2-inch (5 cm) bunches of pearly everlasting and hot-glue them around the inside opening of the wreath. Hot-glue the orange slices to the wreath, placing them between the pomegranates in the center ring and between the flowers in the inner ring. Finally, hot-glue the nandina berries around all three rings.

Silver White Wreath

Materials: *9-inch (23 cm) straw base, tulle, chenille craft stem (pipe cleaner), silver gray artemisia, white annual statice, baby's-breath, money plant, straight pins, floral picks, floral pins, glue gun*

Although this step is optional, wrapping the base with tulle (very fine netting) makes a neat wreath back and prevents the base from shedding small pieces of straw. Secure both ends with straight pins. Wrap the chenille stem around the base and twist the ends into a loop for hanging.

Form small bunches of artemisia—about three 3-inch (8 cm) stems each—and pick them around the inside of the base, overlapping the stems of one bunch with the foliage of the next. Pick fuller and longer bunches of artemisia around the outside of the base, so that the foliage extends in a feathery halo.

Form small bouquets of white flowers—each one a cluster of statice surrounded by delicate baby's-breath—and pin them into place around the base. Hot-glue stems of the round money plant into the wreath, filling in any holes.

Red and Gold Wreath

Materials: *21-inch (53 cm) grapevine base, artificial grapes, assorted pods, eucalyptus leaves, dried pomegranates, preserved ferns, gold craft angel, red silk roses, poppy seedheads, artificial berries, 6 yards (5.5 m) wired burgundy ribbon 2 inches (5 cm) wide, gold spray paint, glue gun, spool wire*

Spray-paint the grapes and pods thoroughly, the eucalyptus leaves and pomegranates lightly. Set aside to dry.

Hot-glue the ferns to the back of the base, as shown. The tips should point outward and, on the sides, slightly upward. Add some fronds to the inside circle. Hot-glue the angel to one side.

Lay the roses, pomegranates, pods, poppy seedheads, eucalyptus leaves, and grapes around the wreath so that each type of material is evenly distributed. Hot-glue the materials to the base in clusters, keeping the work as symmetrical as possible. Fill in empty spots with berries and extra grapes.

Cut off a 5-foot (1.5 m) piece of ribbon and form it into a 5-loop bow. Wire it together and set aside. Loop the remaining ribbon back and forth across the front of the base, tucking it behind large items and hot-gluing it in place. Hot-glue the bow to the top center.

Holiday Garland

Materials: *9-foot (2.7 m)
artificial evergreen garland;
preserved cedar; juniper with
berries attached; 3 yards (2.7 m)
of gold mesh ribbon 3 inches
(8 cm) wide; 9 feet of green and
gold brocade ribbon 3 inches
wide; wired gold beading; magnolia leaves; pinecones; gilded
holly leaves; dried hydrangeas;
dried blue larkspur; dried lavender flowers; spool wire; glue gun*

To make a full, lush garland,
attach some materials to the back,
for a three-dimensional look, and
apply all materials in groupings,
rather than as single items here
and there. Find the center of the
garland. Then, as you proceed,
attach all materials so that they
point outward from the center.

First wire the cedar and juniper to the base, covering it completely. Form a bow with the gold ribbon, wire it to the center of the base, and drape the streamers along each side, wiring them on in several places. Repeat with the brocade ribbon and the gold beads. Hot-glue the magnolia leaves to the garland, positioning them in groups of three. Wire clusters of pinecones together, then wire them to the garland. Hot-glue the holly, hydrangeas, larkspur, and lavender in place.

Flowers and Twigs

Materials: *wire ring base; small, branched twigs; dried red roses; dried white, pink, and purple annual statice; small sprigs of pepperberries or craft berries; artificial pussy willows; lichens; spool floral wire; glue gun*

To make this unusual wreath, start with small, graceful, branched twigs, preferably with a few lichens attached.

Cut the twigs 3 to 5 inches (7 to 12 cm) long, trimming them on the thick end so that you retain the branched portions. Wire the twigs together in bunches by the thick ends, then wire the bunches to the wire ring base, positioning the top of each new bunch over the wires of the previous one.

Hot-glue short stems of dried flowers and lichens into the twigs.

Crab Apples and Galax

Materials: *straw base, Spanish moss, galax leaves, crab apples, red-dyed baby's-breath, narrow red ribbon, floral pins, floral picks, precut lengths of floral wire, vegetable oil*

Although you can purchase a moss-covered base for this wreath, it will be prettier if you make your own—looser and fluffier, with more wispy strands.

Cover the base with handfuls of Spanish moss, attaching them with floral pins. Attach groups of three galax leaves to floral picks, arranging the leaves in a clover design, and pick them evenly around the wreath.

Insert a piece of floral wire through each crab apple, positioning it near the bottom, and wrap each wire around a pick. Pick the apples into the base.

Pick in small bunches of red baby's-breath. Make a multi-loop bow from the ribbon and pin it into place. Finally, rub a bit of vegetable oil onto the leaves and apples.

Culinary Wreaths

Culinary Christmas Wreath

Materials: *grapevine base, silk sunflowers, dried pomegranates, dried quince slices, dried apple slices, hot red peppers, millet heads, amaranth flowers, Sweet Annie, silver king artemisia, safflowers, lemon mint, cinnamon sticks, tansy flowers, dried grapefruit slice, glue gun*

To make this lush, full wreath, hot-glue all materials to a grapevine base in the order listed, using a great deal of glue if necessary. It's helpful to apply the heavy items first, then the light, fragile ones. On the wreath shown, the materials are arranged in random clusters.

To help you tell which material is which, here's what the uncommon ones look like. Dried quince slices are red-orange and resemble tomato slices. Millet heads resemble beige foxtails. Amaranth blooms are long, fuzzy, and burgundy red. Sweet Annie is a reddish brown grain; artemisia is silver and lacy. Safflowers are orange and clover-like. Lemon mint contributes the dried leaves and the lavender flowers. Tansy flowers are clusters of small yellow buttons.

Raffia-Wrapped Vegetables

Materials: *three 8-inch (20 cm) grapevine bases, 1 hank natural raffia, juniper sprigs, hemlock sprigs, green beans, asparagus, radishes (including stems), almonds, hazelnuts, pearl onions, dried japonica berries, spool wire, glue gun*

First wire the three bases together. To conceal the wired areas, wrap several strands of raffia over them, ending with a knot in front.

Hot-glue the juniper and hemlock sprigs to the wreath, as shown in the photo. Make three bundles of vegetables, with some green beans, asparagus, and radishes in each one. Tie the bundles to the wreath with raffia, knotting it in front.

Hot-glue the nuts, onions, and berries around the vegetables.

Red Grapes and Apples

Materials: *straw base, magnolia leaves, red grapes, red and green apples, oranges, cinnamon sticks, floral picks, precut lengths of floral wire, floral pins, glue gun*

Fruit makes for a heavy wreath, so you'll need a heavy wire hanger and a secure nail. Alternatively, use this one as a table wreath, for an arresting holiday centerpiece, perhaps with a group of wide candles in the center.

Attach each magnolia leaf to a pick and insert the picked leaves around the outside and the inside of the base in a spiral pattern. Then add bunches of grapes, attaching them with floral pins. If you need larger pins, bend pieces of floral wire into hairpin shapes. Remove the wires from some floral picks, impale the apples and oranges on the picks, and insert them randomly around the wreath. Hot-glue the cinnamon sticks to picks and position them around the wreath, or hot-glue the cinnamon directly to the wreath.

Materials: *purchased garlic swag, rosemary sprigs (or any delicate evergreen foliage), scarlet globe amaranth flowers, wired-cord ribbon, glue gun*

Garlic swags are widely available at kitchen specialty shops. To dress one up for Christmas, hot-glue sprigs of rosemary and red globe amaranth among the garlic bulbs. If you don't have access to these materials, any delicate green foliage and small, dried, red flowers will work.

Make a bow of red wired cord, wrapping the streamers around a pencil in several places to form loops. Hang the festive swag in your own kitchen or delight a good cook with a unique Christmas gift.

Garlic Swag

Golden Wheat Wreath

Materials: *purchased wheat base (or straw base, stalks of wheat, and floral pins), preserved cedar, Sweet Annie, eucalyptus leaves, pinecones, nigella pods, glue gun*

Ready-made bases of wheat are available at many craft stores. If you need to make your own, first trim the stalks of wheat to about 8 inches (20 cm) long including the seedhead, and soak the stalks in water for at least 1 hour, until they're pliable and easy to work with. Wire small bunches of wheat together, then pin them onto the straw base, pointing all the seedheads counterclockwise and positioning the heads of each bunch over the stalks of the previous bunch, to produce a spiral design. Allow to dry.

Hot-glue the remaining materials into the wreath in clusters, angling them all counterclockwise. Working one stem at a time, apply a generous dollop of glue to the stem end, insert it into the base, and hold the stem in position a few seconds, until the glue sets. Begin with the cedar, then the reddish brown Sweet Annie, then the eucalyptus leaves and pinecones, and finally the striped nigella pods.

Crisscrossed Ribbons

Materials: *straw base, 6 yards (5.5 m) of red velvet ribbon 1 inch (2.5 cm) wide, 4 yards of green satin ribbon 3/4 inch (19 mm) wide, straight pins or hot glue, real or artificial evergreen sprigs, pinecones, floral picks, floral wire, floral pin*

Various widths of ribbon would work well for this wreath, as long as the green is narrower than the red.

Wrap the red ribbon around the base in a crisscross pattern, securing the ends with straight pins or hot glue.

Pick small branches of evergreens into the base in the pattern shown. Wire each cone to a pick and insert them, as well. Finally, make a multi-loop bow with both ribbons, leaving long streamers, and wire it around the center. Use a long floral pin to pin the bow to the base.

Cinnamon Lattice

Materials: *8-inch (20 cm) grapevine base, 8 long cinnamon sticks, coccinea flower (or other large, exotic bloom), garden moss, small dried pomegranates, artificial grapes, pinecone, dried hydrangea flowers, white bunnytails, 1-1/2 yards (1.4 m) gold web ribbon 2 inches (5 cm) wide, glue gun*

First make the cinnamon-stick lattice. Lay four cinnamon sticks diagonally across the back of the vine base, all going in one direction. Lay the remaining cinnamon diagonally in the opposite direction, so that they form a diamond pattern with the first. Cut all the cinnamon to fit and hot-glue to the vine base.

Position the coccinea flower at the bottom of the base and hot-glue it in place. Hot-glue pieces of moss randomly around the front until about half the base is covered, leaving spaces between the moss pieces. Hot-glue the pomegranates in the spaces, directly to the vine base, then add the grapes and the pinecone. Fill in the wreath with bits of hydrangea, hot-gluing them in place. Add a few bunnytails at the bottom.

Loop the ribbon back and forth across the front of the wreath, tucking it in among the materials and hot-gluing it behind major pieces.

Wicker and Yarrow

Materials: *8-inch (20 cm) green wicker base, 9 yards (8 m) of printed ribbon 1 inch (2.5 cm) wide, 16 to 20 sprigs of red-dyed yarrow, spool wire, glue gun*

Cut the ribbon into six pieces 1-1/2 yards long and make a bow from each piece, wiring each bow across the center. Hot-glue the bows onto the wicker base in a large cluster.

Trim the yarrow sprigs to workable lengths. Cover the stem end of one sprig with hot-glue and insert it into the bows. Repeat with the remaining yarrow.

Wassail Wreath

Materials: *straw base, corks, red canella berries, hemlock cones, purchased multi-loop bow or 4 yards (3.7 m) of plaid ribbon 1 inch (2.5 cm) wide, sprigs of evergreens, glue gun, floral picks, floral wire*

Hot-glue the corks onto the straw base at various angles, covering it completely. Then hot-glue the hemlock cones and canella berries onto the corks, distributing them evenly around the wreath.

Form bundles of evergreen sprigs, fasten each bundle to a pick, and pick the evergreens into the wreath, as shown in the photo. Make a bow and wire it to the bottom center of the wreath.

Cinnamon-Scented Wreath

Materials: *cinnamon-covered foam base, 4 yards (3.7 m) of printed cotton ribbon 1-1/2 inches (4 cm) wide, sprigs of fresh or artificial pine, cinnamon sticks, dried flowers (pepper grass, German statice, white annual statice), pinecone, brown craft berries, spool wire, floral picks, glue gun*

Every Christmas, bases covered with crushed cinnamon appear in craft stores. Incredibly fragrant, they can make the whole house smell like Christmas.

To begin, make a large bow, wire it around the center, and wire the bow to the base.

To create the top arrangement, pick stems of pine around the bow. Hot-glue cinnamon sticks among the pine, then hot-glue the dried flowers around the arrangement to fill in the design.

To make the bottom arrangement, use similar methods and materials, but replace the bow with a pinecone and a spray of berries.

Woodland Fawn

Materials: *8-inch (20 cm) vine base, four 10- to 12-inch (25 to 30 cm) pieces of contorted filbert or twisted vine, small pieces of green moss, craft deer, preserved cedar, 1 stem of artificial berries, glue gun*

Hot-glue the pieces of filbert or twisted vine onto the wreath base, so that they project from the base in three directions, as shown in the photo.

While the glue is still warm, cover it with pieces of moss. Glue the deer into the bottom of the base. Glue the cedar in place, positioning the sprigs so that they curve upward and inward. Cut the stem of berries into several smaller clusters and hot-glue them in place. Cover any exposed glue with pieces of moss.

Parchment Angel

Materials: *oval grapevine base; lotus pods; thin twigs; parchment angel; stalks of wheat; 1-1/2 yards (1.4 m) of wired ribbon 2 to 3 inches (5 to 8 cm) wide; sprigs of fresh or artificial blue spruce; red eucalyptus leaves; parchment roses; pink craft berries; rat-tail celosia; lichens; gold spray paint; spool wire; glue gun; floral picks; blue, iridescent beading*

First spray-paint the lotus pods and twigs gold and set them aside to dry. Wire the angel to the center of the base. Wire the stalks of wheat together just below the seedheads, then wire the wheat sheaf to the top of the base; reinforce with hot glue. Arrange the ribbon around the base, wiring it on in several places.

Hot-glue the blue spruce to the base, then the eucalyptus, the lotus pods, and the parchment roses. Attach the berries, rat-tail celosia, and gold twigs to floral picks and pick them into the base. Hot-glue the lichens around the base. Finally, drape the beads around the top and attach them with a dab of hot glue.

Bird's Nests and Greenery

Materials: *straw base, garden moss, alder twigs (or other thin twigs, preferably with seedpods attached), magnolia or laurel leaves and small branches, galax leaves, Virginia pinecones, 4 yards (3.7 m) of wired green ribbon 1 inch (2.5 cm) wide with gold border, craft bird's nests, crab apples, floral pins, spool wire, floral picks*

Cover the base completely with moss, attaching it with floral pins. Pin the twigs to the back of the base, so that they project outward from the edge in a spiral pattern.

Arrange the remaining materials in three large groupings. First pin the magnolia leaves and branches to the base, then pick in the galax leaves and pinecones. Make a bow, wire it around the center, and pin it in place, allowing the streamers to curl around the base.

Insert a piece of wire through each bird's nest, positioning it toward the bottom; wire the nests to floral picks and pick the nests into the base. Finally, remove the wire from some floral picks, impale the crab apples on the blunt ends, and insert the pointed ends into the wreath.

Cottage in the Woods

Materials: twig base; garden moss; sponge mushroom; craft twig house; tiny red beads, or red paint and fine-tipped paintbrush; yellow paint; silver glitter fabric paint; tiny jingle bells; tiny plastic or paper snowflake; glue gun; scissors

Hot-glue small pieces of moss around the twig base. Using the scissors, cut the mushroom to fit snugly against the wreath and glue it into position, flat side up.

Decorate the cottage as shown, with either tiny red beads (hot-glue them in place) or dabs of red paint. Put a candle in the window by painting the tip of a tiny twig yellow and hot-gluing it to the window. Dab bits of the silver glitter paint on the twig base, around the cottage, and on the roof; drip some off the front step and the edge of the mushroom to form icicles.

When the paint is dry, hot-glue the cottage onto the mushroom. Hot-glue the bells and the snowflake to nearby twigs.

Nautical Teddy Bear

Materials: *8-inch (20 cm) grapevine base; 6 white-washed twigs, 1 as long as the diameter of the base, 5 half as long; teddy bear; dried blue statice; gold plastic stars; 2-inch (5 cm) grapevine mini-wreath; 4 tiny pinecones; red cording; red acrylic paint; small paintbrush or cotton swab; toy boat; 12 small marbles and 1 large marble; glue gun; spool wire*

Working on the back of the 8-inch base, hot-glue the long twig across the center of the base. Then hot-glue the five short twigs on one half of the base, so that they radiate from the center, as shown. Wire the bear to the base.

Hot-glue the blue statice around the base in a pointed, starburst pattern. Then hot-glue the stars around the wreath, hanging some from the vine tendrils, placing others in the flowers.

Wrap the red cording around the mini-wreath, ending with a simple two-loop bow. Hot-glue the pinecones under the bow. Dot the mini-wreath with red paint and glue it to the twigs, as shown.

Glue the boat in place to help balance the arrangement; hot-glue the marbles around the boat to create waves.

Contributing Designers

Julianne Bronder is a floral designer and interior design consultant. Pages 14, 17, 52.

Janet Frye is the owner of The Enchanted Florist in Arden, North Carolina. Pages 12, 20, 50, 54.

Fred Tyson Gaylor is a product designer for Hanford's, a wholesale holiday accessory company in Charlotte, North Carolina. Pages 30, 44.

Cynthia Gillooley is the owner of The Golden Cricket in Asheville, North Carolina. Pages 38, 56.

Judy Horn is the owner of The Corn Husk Shoppe in Asheville, North Carolina. Page 48.

Josena McCaig, formerly a floral designer for the Biltmore Estate, operates her own floral design studio, "Some Parlor Ivy," in Asheville, North Carolina. Pages 18, 28, 34, 42.

Alyce Nadeau operates Goldenrod Mountain Herb Farm in Deep Gap, North Carolina. Pages 22, 24.

Diane Weaver is an artist, author, and craft designer from Weaverville, North Carolina. Pages 26, 40, 46, 60, 62.

And thanks to Martha Borawa (page 32), Clara Curtis (page 58), Beth Hohensee (page 36), and Claudette Mautor (page 16).

Index